I0479454

Artificial Intelligence For Non-Techies: How to Pivot & Push Using AI For Business

Natina Marie Hill

FOR NON-TECHIES VOL.1

PEN**HAUS**
MEDIA

ISBN: 9798324831226

Dedicated to all the multi-hyphenate creatives, ambitious "over-achieving" entrepreneurs, and my full circle of melanin muses.

For Madea and our tribe.
Nadia, my world peace baby.
Diallo, my forever love.
Doc, my creative inspiration resting in paradise.

INTRODUCTION

During my 25-year journey as an entrepreneur and multi-hyphenate creative, I've acquired numerous nicknames, but the one that has endured is "Ask Teeves aka Teeves," lovingly given to me by my high school friends, now family, in our close-knit group known as *The ROC Family*. Within this circle, I'm referred to as Teeves. Let me clarify the origin of this nickname, "Ask Teeves". It all began as a playful joke due to my tendency to be a know-it-all, readily and sometimes awkwardly blurting information on a wide array of topics. More often than not, I happen to be right, a fact my friends acknowledge but enjoy poking fun at endlessly. At times, I may profess knowledge only to discover I'm completely wrong. Nevertheless, I dedicate a substantial amount of time absorbing information from the internet and professional development. I take immense pleasure in sharing knowledge and resources. Over time, I've been dubbed "Lady Google" while my sisters call me "Oprah". More recently, I've been coined as, "The Oracle" inspired by the 1999 film, *The Matrix,* by my husband.

Drawing parallels to Google's predecessor, Ask Jeeves, which launched in beta form in April 1997 and fully debuted on June 1, 1997, the concept revolved around users posing natural-language queries, with the valet providing answers—a precursor to modern generative AI chat tools like Gemini and ChatGPT that we employ today. This brings me to the reason for creating an instructional guide aimed at assisting fellow entrepreneurs and content creators in learning AI-based business tools.

This book marks the first installment of 'For Non-Techies,' a compilation of how-to guides designed to build a community of tech-savvy leaders. The world of AI can be overwhelming for many entrepreneurs I encounter, so the content is intentionally simplified to alleviate the fear associated with working with AI. Additionally, I've included some essential resources, such as an AI Toolkit, to assist you in engaging more deeply with AI, as well as user-friendly GenAI tools.

NATINA MARIE HILL

Natina Marie Hill is a dynamic creative storyteller and seasoned business management consultant. She specializes in workforce development solutions, offering training to bridge the skill gaps in digital and technology. Natina brings a unique blend of business acumen, technical skills, and content creation prowess.

With a rich educational background and a 25-year entrepreneurial journey, she serves as the CEO of Hill Consulting Firm. Additionally, as the Founder of PenHaus Media, Natina Marie writes, directs, and executive produces film and TV projects. Passionate about elevating Black women's stories, she curates the melanin muse® weekly love letter and hosts *The Pivot Muse* podcast, where she shares stories and offers advice from global professionals on making one of life's most important decisions
– **the pivot.**

Natina enjoys traveling and crafting creative recipes to host dinners with her family and friends. Be sure to subscribe to melanin muse® weekly love letter for exclusive perks. Listen to *The Pivot Muse* podcast on Spotify, YouTube, Apple, Amazon, and Audible.

Booking: hello@thepivotmuse.com

Photo credit: Miracle Sturdivant

CONTACT INFO

CONTENTS

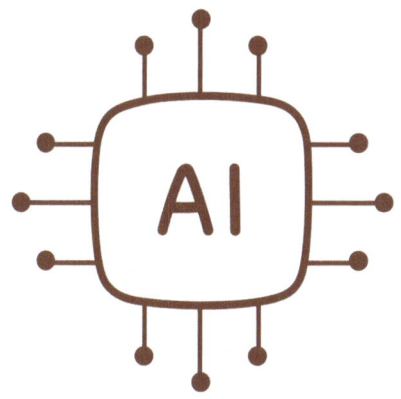

AI UNVEILED

Demystifying AI: What's it all about?

Simply put, AI (Artificial Intelligence) refers to machines or computers mimicking human intelligence to perform tasks.

What AI Does?

AI can learn from data, make decisions, recognize patterns, and even understand human language.

Everyday AI: From voice assistants (Siri and Alexa) to social media algorithms, AI is already part of our lives.

How can AI boost your business?

In this guide, you will discover how AI can help your content creation and entrepreneurial ventures.

Efficiency Boost: AI can automate tasks, saving time and reducing errors.

Personalization: AI can tailor content and recommendations for your audience, boosting engagement.

START SMART WITH AI

Where to begin?

5 Simple Steps to Finding Your AI Path

STEP 1: *Identifying Needs*: Assess your business to spot areas where AI can be helpful.

STEP 2: *AI-Ready Tools*: Research AI tools and platforms that suit your goals.

STEP 3: *Starting Small*: Don't feel pressured to dive into complex AI projects right away.

STEP 4: *AI Toolbox*: What tools are right for you?

Types of AI Tools: Understand the various AI tools like chatbots, content generators, and analytics.

STEP 5: *Tool Selection*: Pick tools that align with your objectives and are user-friendly.

Learning Curve: Choose tools that you and your team can quickly grasp.

Check out the **Resources for Your AI Journey** section in this book to access a curated AI Toolbox for you to get started.

QUESTIONS

- What specific goals are we trying to achieve in the short-term and long-term?

- Are there any challenges or bottlenecks hindering our progress?

- What are the key functions and processes that drive our business operations?

- Are there repetitive and time-consuming tasks that could benefit from automation?

- What types of data do we collect, and where is this data stored?

- Is there valuable data that could be leveraged for insights and decision-making?

- How do we interact with our customers, and through which channels?

- Are there opportunities to enhance customer experiences using AI-driven personalization or chatbots?

- Are we currently analyzing data to gain insights into customer behavior, market trends, or operational efficiency?

- Can AI be used to improve our data analytics processes and uncover hidden patterns?

QUESTIONS

- Which tasks within our organization are repetitive and rule-based?

- Could these tasks be automated to free up employee time for more strategic activities?

- Are there industry-specific regulations or compliance requirements we need to meet?

- Can AI assist in ensuring compliance and data security?

- What are the common pain points or issues customers encounter in their interactions with us?

- Can AI-powered solutions address these pain points and improve customer satisfaction?

- What is our budget and resource availability for implementing AI projects?

- Are there limitations that need to be considered when planning AI initiatives?

- What AI trends and technologies are emerging in our industry?

- What are our short-term and long-term AI goals?

AI GOALS

WHEN SETTING YOUR AI GOALS, MAKE SURE IT FOLLOWS THE SMART STRUCTURE. USE THE QUESTIONS BELOW TO CREATE YOUR GOALS.

S	SPECIFIC WHAT DO I WANT TO ACCOMPLISH?	
M	MEASURABLE HOW WILL I KNOW WHEN IT IS ACCOMPLISHED?	
A	ACHIEVABLE HOW CAN THE GOAL BE ACCOMPLISHED?	
R	RELEVANT DOES THIS SEEM WORTHWHILE?	
T	TIME BOUND WHEN CAN I ACCOMPLISH THIS GOAL?	

BRAINSTORMING

ACTION BRAINSTORMING CAN HELP IDENTIFY WHAT THINGS ARE HELPING OR STOPPING YOU FROM ACHIEVING YOUR GOALS.

GOAL

STOP DOING

DO LESS OF

KEEP DOING

DO MORE OF

START DOING

GENAI CONTENT CREATION

Brainstorming Brilliance: Using AI for ideas

Idea Generation: AI can analyze trends and suggest creative content ideas.

Keyword Insights: Discover the best keywords to optimize your content.

Staying Ahead: Stay competitive with AI-driven content strategies.

Crafting with AI: Content creation made easier

AI-Assisted Writing: Use AI to help generate content ideas, headlines, and even full articles. Be sure to read all AI-assisted writing and edit in your voice and tone.

Editing Support: AI can improve grammar, style, and readability.

Time-Saver: Speed up content creation while maintaining quality.

Perfecting Your Pitch: AI-powered content insights

Audience Understanding: AI can analyze audience data for content personalization.

Performance Predictions: AI tools can forecast how well your content may perform.

Continuous Improvement: Use AI insights to refine your content strategy.

ENGAGING AUDIENCES WITH AI

The Personal Touch

Audience Engagement: AI can tailor content to individual preferences.

User Retention: Personalized experiences lead to more engaged and loyal customers.

Chatbots: AI-driven chatbots can provide immediate responses and assistance.

Build Customer Loyalty

AI's ability to process and analyze data at scale, combined with machine learning techniques, enables businesses and organizations to provide highly personalized experiences to their users and customers. This not only enhances user engagement but also fosters customer loyalty and satisfaction.

Recommendations Revolution: AI's role in content suggestions

Content Recommendations: AI can suggest relevant articles, products, or content to users.

Increased Engagement: Users are more likely to interact when content suits their interests.

Implementation Made Easy: Many platforms offer plug-and-play AI recommendation systems.

AUTOMATE TASKS WITH AI

Time-Saving Magic: Automate and Streamline

Incorporating AI automation into your content creation or business processes can yield significant benefits in terms of efficiency and productivity. However, it's essential to approach it strategically, starting small, and gradually expanding while keeping ethical considerations in mind.

Why Automate Routine Tasks?

Automation Benefits: AI can automate repetitive tasks, such as data entry and scheduling.

Efficiency Gains: Save time and reduce errors by letting AI handle routine work.

Simple Steps: Most automation tools are user-friendly and require minimal setup.

Getting Started with AI Automation

Identifying Opportunities: Determine which tasks can be automated in your business.

Tool Selection: Choose automation tools that match your needs and integrate easily. Check out our curated toolbox in the resources.

Action Steps:

- Create a detailed list of your daily, weekly, and monthly tasks.
- Choose a specific task or process to automate first, such as scheduling social media posts or automating email responses.
- Test the automation before publishing.

TASK LIST INVENTORY

M T W T F

DAILY

MONTHLY:

DATA AND AI

What is Data?

In simple terms, data refers to pieces of information or facts that are collected, stored, and used for various purposes. Data can take many forms, such as numbers, text, images, or even sounds. It's like the building blocks of information that organizations use to make decisions, track performance, and understand their operations.

Examples:

AI is running on our smartphones helping to take better photos and add special effects. AI is creating those beautiful curated videos and slideshows automatically on your smartphone.

AI-powered chatbots can gather customer feedback and inquiries, and then personalize responses making us feel like we are speaking to a human.

How can AI help manage data?

Data Collection:
AI can automate the collection of data from various sources, including sensors, websites, and social media.

Data Cleansing:
AI can clean and preprocess data by detecting and correcting errors, duplicates, and inconsistencies.

Automation of Tasks:
AI automates repetitive data-related tasks, such as data entry, data validation, and report generation, freeing up human resources for more strategic activities.

Data Analysis:
AI algorithms can analyze large datasets quickly and identify patterns, trends, and insights that would be challenging or impossible for humans to discern.

Data Storage and Retrieval:
AI-driven databases and data management systems can efficiently store, organize, and retrieve data.

Data Handling: Keeping It Secure and Private

Data Privacy: Protect user data and respect privacy regulations.

Security Measures: Implement encryption and access controls for data protection.

Responsible Data Management: Safeguard data against breaches and misuse.

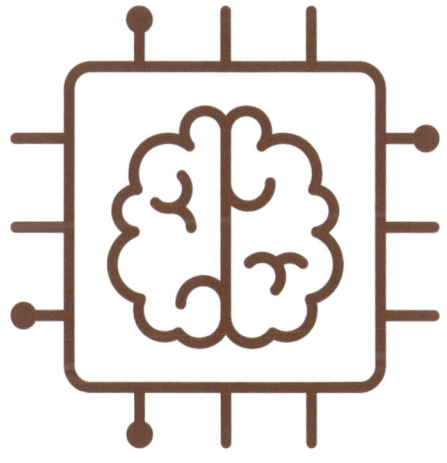

AI's Best Friend: The Importance of Data

Data's Role: Understand that AI relies on data to function effectively.

Collecting Data: Learn how to gather data that's relevant to your AI project.

Quality Matters: Ensure data is accurate and complete for reliable AI results.

Data Preparation and Integration:

Most AI automation relies on data. Ensure your data is clean, organized, and accessible for automation tools to work effectively.

RESOURCES
FOR
YOUR
AI JOURNEY

NO CODE APPS

1. **Adalo:** Adalo is a no-code platform that makes creating apps as easy as putting together a slide deck. You can create interactive components, set up databases for storing information, and integrate with various APIs to extend your app's functionality. Adalo is great for building mobile and web apps and allows you to publish directly to iOS, Android, and the web.

2. **Bubble:** Bubble is a powerful no-code platform for web applications, suitable for everything from simple prototypes to complex, data-driven software. It features a visual interface for designing your app and logic, a built-in database solution, and the ability to include custom JavaScript and integrate APIs for advanced needs.

3. **OutSystems:** OutSystems is a low-code platform that's more targeted at enterprise-level applications, but can certainly be used for smaller projects. It provides a visual development environment, one-click deployment, and the ability to integrate with existing systems and databases. OutSystems has a focus on scalability and security, which is great for business applications.

4. **Appgyver:** Appgyver is a no-code platform that allows you to build apps for all platforms, including web, iOS, Android, and even wearable devices. It offers a drag-and-drop interface for designing your app, a visual logic builder, a database builder, and the ability to integrate APIs. It's also known for its powerful composition tool that allows for a high level of customization.

5. **Glide:** Glide is a unique no-code tool that allows you to create mobile apps directly from Google Sheets, making it an excellent choice for simple apps that are primarily data-driven. It's intuitive, straightforward, and a great option if you're just starting out in the world of app development.

6. **Webflow:** While Webflow is primarily a website builder, its powerful visual CSS and interactions tools make it a strong contender for certain types of web applications. It integrates well with various databases and APIs, and it's a solid choice if you want your application to have a high degree of visual polish.

AI TOOLS FOR CONTENT CREATION

1. Content Generation:

Copy.ai: Generates marketing copy, product descriptions, and more with AI.

2. Chatbots and Conversational AI:

ChatGPT by OpenAI: Create chatbots and conversational agents without coding.

Landbot: No-code chatbot builder for websites and messaging apps.

3. Marketing and Customer Engagement:

Outgrow: Create interactive content, quizzes, and calculators to engage audiences.

Revoice: Generates voiceovers for videos and marketing content.

4. Data Analytics and Visualization:

Tableau Public: A no-code data visualization tool for creating interactive charts and dashboards.

Google Data Studio: Easily create and share interactive reports and dashboards.

5. AI Automation and Workflow:

Zapier: Automate tasks and connect different apps and services without coding.

Integromat: A no-code automation platform similar to Zapier but with more complex workflows.

6. Natural Language Processing (NLP):

MonkeyLearn: Build custom text analysis models for sentiment analysis, topic classification, and more.

Text Blaze: Automate and accelerate typing with text snippets and templates.

7. Design and Creative Content:

Crello: A graphic design tool for creating social media graphics, posters, and more.

Canva: Offers a wide range of design templates for various purposes.

8. E-commerce and Sales:

Shopify: Create and customize online stores with no coding required.
Salesforce Essentials: CRM and sales automation for small businesses.

Printify: Provides a vast selection of products and works with multiple e-commerce platforms, such as Shopify, to help you create and sell custom merchandise.

Scalable Press: A platform catering to businesses and entrepreneurs looking for custom apparel and merchandise, offering a variety of printing options.

9. AI-Powered SEO:

Clearscope: Analyze top-performing content and optimize your content for search engines.

Surfer SEO: Optimize your content for search engines with AI-driven recommendations.

10. Voice and Speech Recognition:

AssemblyAI: Convert spoken language into written text for transcription and voice recognition.

Crisp.ai: Improve audio quality and reduce background noise in recordings.

AI TOOLS FOR VIDEO & AUDIO

1. Video Creation:

Lumen5: Converts text content into engaging video presentations with AI-generated visuals.

InVideo: An online video creation platform that uses AI for text-to-video conversion.

2. Video Editing:

Veed.io: An AI-powered video editing tool that makes editing and creating video content simple.

Magisto: An AI-powered video editor that automates the video creation process.

Clipchamp: A no-code video editing platform with AI-driven features for quick edits.

3. Voiceover, and Dubbing:

Descript: An AI-powered transcription and voice editing tool for video and audio content.

Synthetic Voices by Google Cloud: Create synthetic voices for narrations and dubbing.

4. Video Enhancement:

Vibby: A platform for annotating and enhancing videos with AI-powered features.

Topaz Video Enhance AI: Enhance video quality, upscale resolution, and reduce noise.

5. Stock Footage and Media:

Artgrid: Access a library of high-quality stock footage for video projects.

Pexels Videos: Offers free stock videos with a wide variety of clips.

6. Visual Effects and Animation:

Rendrfx: Create animations, motion graphics, and visual effects with ease.

Blender: A free and open-source 3D content creation suite for advanced animation.

7. Subtitles and Captioning:

Rev.com: Offers automated transcription and captioning services for videos.

SubtitleBee: A tool for generating and editing subtitles for video content.

Captions.ai: Create studio-grade videos in a few taps and correct eye contact in post-production.

8. Video Analytics:

Wistia: Provides video hosting and analytics to understand viewer engagement.

Vidyard: Analyzes video performance and user interactions with AI insights.

9. AI-Powered Video SEO:

TubeBuddy: A YouTube-certified browser extension for video optimization with AI insights.

Morningfame: Helps YouTubers optimize their content strategy with AI recommendations.

10. Podcasting and Editing Audio:

SquadCast/Descript: Transfer Squadcast recordings and files quickly using the "Edit in Descript" integration.

Riverside/Spotify for Podcasters: You can record high-quality, collaborative audio and video podcasts in Riverside and publish them seamlessly in Spotify for Podcasters.

BUILD YOUR AI TOOLKIT

Select Three Essential AI Tools & Related Projects or Tasks

BUDGETING FOR AI

Dollars and Sense: Planning your AI Budget

It is essential to understand the costs associated with AI integration. Consider what tools you can use for free and which tools will bring more bang for your buck (ROI). Allocate resources based on your budget to maximize AI's impact.

Cost Considerations:

Identify expenses like software, hardware, and personnel.

Define Success:

Set clear objectives for your AI projects. Track and measure AI's impact on your business.

AI TOOL #1

MONTHLY FEE: $

ANNUAL FEE: $

AI TOOL #2

MONTHLY FEE: $

ANNUAL FEE: $

AI TOOL #3

MONTHLY FEE: $

ANNUAL FEE: $

TOTAL BUDGET: $

Long-Term Benefits:

Consider how AI can create lasting value for your business.

GLOSSARY

Artificial Intelligence (AI): The simulation of human intelligence in machines that can perform tasks that typically require human intelligence, such as problem-solving, learning, and decision-making.

Generative AI (GenAI): A type of artificial intelligence (AI) that creates new content based on data it has been trained on.

Machine Learning (ML): A subset of AI that enables machines to learn and improve from experience without being explicitly programmed, often using statistical techniques.

Natural Language Processing (NLP): The branch of AI that focuses on the interaction between computers and human language, enabling machines to understand, interpret, and generate human language.

Chatbot: A computer program or AI application that can simulate conversation with human users, often used for customer support and interactions.

Data Analytics: The process of examining, cleaning, transforming, and interpreting data to extract valuable insights and support decision-making.

Personalization: The customization of content, products, or services based on individual user preferences and behavior.

Algorithm: A set of rules or instructions followed by a computer to perform a specific task or solve a particular problem.

Automation: The use of technology, such as AI and robots, to perform tasks and processes with minimal human intervention.

Workflow: The sequence of steps or tasks involved in a business process, often automated using AI.

Virtual Assistant: A digital or AI-based assistant that can perform tasks, answer questions, and provide information to users.

ROI (Return on Investment): A measure of the profitability or value generated by an investment, including AI initiatives.

Bias: Systematic and unfair discrimination or favoritism in AI algorithms, often based on race, gender, or other attributes.

Ethical AI: The practice of developing and using AI systems in a way that aligns with ethical principles, fairness, and societal values.

NOTES

NOTES

CONGRATULATIONS!

Congratulations on completing 'Artificial Intelligence For Non-Techies'! You've conquered the first step into the world of AI, demystified its complexities, and now hold the key to scaling your business to new heights.

Embrace this new journey with confidence, knowing that AI is no longer a mystery but a powerful tool in your toolkit. Here's to your continued success and growth!

Tune into 'The Pivot Muse' podcast hosted by Natina Marie for real, raw, and relatable conversations about life and career transitions. Get curated stories and advice from global professionals on making one of life's most important decisions – **the pivot.** 'The Pivot Muse' podcast is available on Spotify, Apple, YouTube, Amazon, and Audible.

Website: thepivotmuse.com
Email: hello@thepivotmuse.com

CONTACT INFO